The Masquerade Ball

The Masquerade Ball

VS Bryant

Library of Congress Control Number: 2011907173
ISBN: Hardcover   978-1-4628-6828-5
                  Softcover   978-1-4628-6827-8
                  Ebook   978-1-4628-6829-2

To order additional copies of this book, contact:
Xlibris Corporation
1-888-795-4274
www.Xlibris.com
Orders@Xlibris.com
90570

Table of Contents

I. Love.

II.   Life

III. *Dreams*

This book is dedicated to God for giving me my talent and placing me on this earth, then for my mom; God rest her soul for always loving what I do and being my greatest fan. Lastly to my two beautiful girls, since birth they have been my greatest inspiration. They are the reason why I keep pushing and will continue to write until the complete story is told.

Love.

LIFE

Love Infinitely For Everything
This is what two small eyes showed me.
Their small voices said to me; see the beauty within, not ugliest flowing in the wind.
Two tiny hands full of devotion & compassion.
Tender heart bigger then wide oceans.

Live Incredibly For Ever
This tiny kick gives hope to a brighter future.
The soft heartbeat, like thunder roaring through a noisy crowd.
This womb expands, so this life can grow, smiles and laughter, so happy to show.

Little Incredibility Future Excitement
Little eyes, small voices, tiny hands, a tender heart . . .
Nysayia my greatest achievement.
Tiny kicks, soft heartbeat, a changing body . . . my new precious gift.
My greatest accomplishments . . . my children.

THE END

A dedication for the one that is here and the one the is coming

6/26/06

What Is Love

Love is,
>   Pain . . . pleasure
>>   Heartache . . . heated passion
>   Deceit . . . devotion

Love is,
>   Compassionate . . . corruptive
>>   Giving . . . taking
>   Sharing . . . controlling

Love is,
>   Hating . . . caring
>>   Mean . . . sensitive
>   Short . . . endless

Love is something wild and untamed.
It's mesmerizing and incredible, a thing to claim.
Love is pain and sorrow as well as pleasure and seductive.
It's something lasting and a gift unmatched by any means.
Its family and friends, lover and things.
Its devotion and compassion, giving and taking.
Yes sometimes it's pain and deceit, heartache and simple mean.
But usually it's a captivating spell, a potion that awakens senses never known to man.
Most important it's you, the one I love; the one that makes me happy, the one that makes me sad, the one I'm truly devoted to and that's truly compassionate to me.
Sometimes you give me heartache and other times it's pleasure.
Yet at the end of the day I wouldn't trade you in anyway.
For nothing in my life is more important to me then you are right now.
You're my passion and devotion, pleasure and pain.
You're my heartache and heartbreak, but one things true you will always be what love means to me.

98'

Faithful

How can eight simple letters have such a big part in
two people's lives?

It's just like birds would not fly without feathers, but
would they die.

I have always said I wanted the simplest of things.

Someone to be with me forever through any type of
weather and one day give me his special rings.

We could grow in time together as one build up our
vines, which would brighten up the sun.

He for me and me for he together we will always be.

Through the storms, the tears, and the raindrops we will
storm with tears of love drops . . .

98'

<u>Mental Love Making</u>

He makes love to my soul & seduces my mind;
the erotic conversations he throws at me,
sensually arousing my psyche & stimulating
my heart, as well as my body.

He caresses me deeply with words silently
spoken, the tantalizing thoughts, he gives causes
me to contemplate, while they burn inside,
letting my words erupt all over the page.

He arouses my mental passion slowly, very
slowly, licking intellectual thoughts from me
yes, from me.

All his wisdom flows through me, penetrating
my very soul, so we can start the next phase.

Holding me tightly & oh so very close driving
me insane through my feet, head, & throat.

Love making at it's very best, pleasing not only
the body, but also the mind & soul.

Love at the highest level, standing up through
all that would have it fall.

He & me; perfection, perfectly
Love everlasting . . .
Lovemaking for eternity . . .

8-27-99

The Love Letter

Dear Love,

As the time glides by my feelings for you rise.

Your tender touch and soft smile made my soul come, long before my body had to decide.

The passionate glares from your caring eyes make my heart sing sweeter than the angels above.

Suddenly and completely I realize and see what you truly mean to me; passion, love, a sweet delicacy.

This is better than my wildest dream, romantic possibilities the best of the best and nothing less.

An ecstasy far better than the drug, like absolute vodka always making me hot.

A love affair that surpasses the heavens.

A seductive dimension that those beneath us can't reach.

My heart and soul I care for you so.

So to you
With Love
From me.

Summer 99'

For Thou Art My Love . . .

for thou are my love
my heart and soul.
the heavens opened up and
sent its most precious
angel for me to love and hold.

I had a dream much more like a fantasy everyone tried to have what I had, but still I didn't see.

Romance at day and passion through the night yet still I didn't realize everything had always been just right.

He treated me like a goddess, but I couldn't do the same.

I treated him so bad and now I feel oh so ashamed.

If I could have just one night to make a change.

I would right the wrongs and always cherish my lover's name.

Emotionless love is what I gave, along with heartache and misery and all the other bad things that's all the same.

If you are listening please give me a chance to mend your heart and love you the same as you did once on lover's lane . . .

97'
Revised 1/6/2011

Passion

Last night I was with him and everything was right,
we kissed and we hugged and he held me so tight.

We had a candle light dinner that was oh so nice and
then played slow music and danced in the dim light.

We danced and we dipped, we kissed and he licked.

He massaged all the right spots and gently kisses them
to make them hot.

I felt my heart in my legs as I came on the bed pane.

He slowly embraced me with all his manly power, I
moaned and I groaned as it slowly started to shower.

I called his name as he called mine, we were making
love for the very first time.

We did everything to please each other that night, we
touched, we pinched, we picked and we bent.

Massages that soothed and fine wine that cooled.

He said, "I love you," I said, "I love you too".

I kissed him and then said good night boo . . .

97'

A Real Man

Through these years I have seen many boys.

All broken up in many forms, some play with guns, others with toys.

But in all my years I haven't seen a real man.

One that works hard for his children and wife, doing all that he can.

A real man never runs away he stands his ground through the sunny and the gray days.

He would give his last and his life, for his children and his wife.

A real man gets dirty so his home will always be clean.

A real man is a father not just a daddy.

Besides buying his kids the finest of things, he can also make them happy and fore fill all their needs.

A real man is a lover as well as a fighter.

Making love through the night, fighting the never-ending battle through the day so his family won't suffer the pain and rain.

A real man is many things, but never a liar.

Prides himself on his words and his heart of fire.

A real man knows that his strength is in his home.

A real man shows that he loves and can do for his own.

THAT'S A REAL MAN!

3-12-97

<u>Fly</u>

I.

I fly.
I dance across the sky.
I soar,
I reach for so much more.
I am,
I am what I am.
I see,
I see all that is to be.

II.

You fly,
You fly to the greatest heights.
You soar,
You become so much more.
You are,
You are what you are.
You see,
You see all that is too been seen.

III.

We fly,
We fly together, day and night.
We soar,
We soar through the universe core.
We become,
We become what we always were.
We see,
We see all the beauty in we.

See me,
Be me.

See me as I really am.
See me flow, see me fly,
See my soul in every drop of water that glides by
See my heart in every child's eye

Be me & I'll be you.
Share my pleasures & I'll share your pain.
Let my love surround you & I'll let your life embrace me.
Let us entwine & become one.
Let us take each other's hands & journey to the sun.

See me, I will see you.
Love me, i will love you.
Be in me, I'll be in you.

8-15-98

Simple Put

Your walk, your talks, just the way you move
Send chills down my spine; I shiver from its groove
Your confidence, manliness, the sternness in your voice,
makes me love you, want you, desire you even more
Your dark skin, soft eyes, smooth skin; damn you blow
my mind
You are gorgeous, a god, the greatest of sculptures
flawless by design

The smell of you relaxes me, drawing me closer, making
me need you, wanting to touch you.
Your lips makes me quiver, their touch starts me to
shiver, you yell no, I love you more, I desire you, you
seduce me to my core.
The way your eyes look at me, makes my soul soar, my spirit
wraps around you, becoming you, and I want you more.

So many words can describes how much I love you; so
many thoughts can show I care
So many ways to show my devotion, so many moments
to be with you, so many . . .

Simple put I love you
Simple put I love you

What more can be said

Written for a friend for her love
12/2010

The Heart

Love

Devotion

Understanding

Caring

Pain

Hurt

Devastation

Betrayal

Laugh

Cry

Floating

Heartbroken

Damage

Adore

Life

The Butterfly

I suddenly remember how to truly cry
The rollercoaster turns, twist, and bends
And I continue to float through the air,
softly descending
I remember the moon once played with stars
I remember the rain once sang with the clouds
Quiet loneliness, wraps itself around me
Cocooning my soul in a blanket of
desperateness
Then suddenly I emerge as the beautiful
butterfly
Spreading hope in the face of despair
I once again can fly
You once again will reach the enigmatic high.

Thoughts

I do love you this I know, do you love me, sometimes I feel
it's so.
We were together once, along while ago.
But now we're apart and it still hurts so.
It was like a dream that has now ended.
We had something of a fantasy I swear we could have not
pretended it.
You took my heart but I gave it with open arms.
I thought I had yours, but sometimes I feel I was wrong.
Could it be that we were truly meant to be?
Or am I a fool, the hopeless romantic type you see.
I ponder us like I ponder the rest of my life.
Are you all that I hope for, all that I need.
Now I sit lost and frowning in my own loneliness.
Going crazy over the thought of your gentle kiss.
Will we be together, this time forever?
Or will you finally destroy me, with your loves endeavor.

9-10-98

To the broken hearted,

I hear your cries, I see your tears, and feel your pain.
I stand tall so I may lift you when you fall.
I smile to remind you that the sun always shines.
I will never leave your side, for I'll be your rock when you are too weak to continue the climb.
I am your friend, sister, and all that has ever been.
I will embrace your pain, so you can know peace.
I will bare your tears, so you can once again remember how to smile.
I will hold you and comfort you, protect you and forever love you.

To the broken hearted I am here and forever will I remain to protect you forever and a day.

8/25/09
10AM

<u>Why</u>

Why do I love he who does not love me?
Why do I hold on to a dream that doesn't want to begin?
Why do I sit around and wait for him to come in?
Why do I open my heart and play a game for a prize I can't win?

I fell for a masterpiece some time ago.
A work of art from his hair, to his eyes, to his lips, and even his
toes; I am infatuated with every word that slips from within.
He can hypnotize you with every word from his mouth.
He can seduce you with this certain little gleam from his eyes.
I get chills from memories of his gently tough.
I still remember his lips & fingers caressing my every thought.
To have him would be a victory, a true fantasy.
To love him would be a gift, a true miracle bestowed upon me.
I would hold him through the day and make love to him through
the night.
I would take care of him forever; I'll be his sun & moonlight.

Why do I love he who does not love me?
Why do I hold on to a dream that doesn't want to begin?
Why do I sit around and wait for him to come in?
Why do I open my heart and play a game for a prize I can't win?

With love to my inspiration.

98'
Revised 1/2011

In Awe . . .

I sit in awe . . . at the beauty that surrounds me each and every day I wake. I bow with tear filled eyes at such delights as to see the moon glow against a midnight blue sky and to behold the sun as it burns across the dawn's horizon.

I am in awe . . . at the children that walk with the majesty of the kings and queens that came before. Tiny feet crossing desolate lands, tiny hands healing nations, with small eyes that holds the universe.

I am at awe . . . at the mothers raising leaders and bearing the pains of the world. Brave women, strong women, beautiful women! I see you and I respect you all.

I am in awe . . . at real men carrying the weight of civilization upon their shoulders. Men feeding families, building mountains, conquering the evil's place here to destroy their families.

I am awed . . . by the writer, writing history, speaking truths unknown and never to be forgot. From the artist painting landscapes of purple and blue, pink sunsets and orange waters, I step aside to see your beauty unfold.

I am in awe . . . at the angelic voice of the singer, singing the songs of heaven making the birds cry. From the composer writing the symphonies of the universe only to fully be appreciated by the planets and the stars above.

I am at awe by me, blessed to walk another day amongst the trees. Able to dance once more with Mother Earth and play with the leaves . . . I am awe!

12/14/2010

Space & Time

A second to love you
A minute to be devoted to you
An hour to cherish you
A day to be with you
A week to fall hopelessly for you
A month to know, I want no one but you
A year to be blessed with you
A lifetime to share with you
An eternity to walk beside you
An everlasting ride through an abyss of happiness

A journey through a sea of total bliss
A passionate affair gentle blows in the mist
A seduction of the mind and soul, too precious to risk
A game for the body to behold
A new world, a galaxy of wonders to unfold

Let me show you a universe beyond anything you have ever known
Let me awaken senses never used and introduce you to new sensations
to forever hold
Let me love your mind, and make love to your soul
Let me caress your body, and tell you a tale never told

Be my lover, my friend, my teacher & my man
And I'll be everything you need me to be
So we can be together for an eternity, in this undiscovered land
What the heavens has put together let no man nor woman server
And together we will be, forever and ever

7-17-99
Revised 12/2010

Private thought,
&
Hidden desires

Private thoughts written down **for all to read.**
Secret desires put on paper for curious eyes to see.
Hidden passions made public for a lover to know.
Unknown truths made known for you to grow.

The possibilities are endless when it comes to your mind.
Time stands still and eternity is endless for the lonely kind.
Private desires and secret passions can open doors to a new
and wonderful joy.
While hidden truths and unknown thoughts can be a barrier
for a life of love.
Let go of whatever is holding you back, for love could be
right there standing beside you.
Let go of the past and prepare for today, let go of the pain
and open your heart to happiness.
Breathe in deep and hold your head high, swallow your
pride & watch your spirit fly.

Be strong it's in your soul, and watch you just might find
your real love.

10-2-98

<u>Pain & Love</u>

My pain comes from a longing for something I may
never have.
My pain comes from loving those in my future, present,
and past.
My pain comes from being too scared to say that which
I really feel.
My pain comes from silence and forever knowing that
it's real.

My love came with the moon, and left with the sun.
My love came too soon and now is on the run.
My love played in the game and lost its will to ever remain.
My love wanted to stay, but left, for you were the only
thing it couldn't tame.

My pain is all that is left now, all that remain.
My love is gone with the wind now, to heartbroken to
ever return again.
My pain is paralyzing, agony, and ignorant.
My love is lonely and eternal, but forever heaven sent.
Love & Pain, this is why I am insane.
My pain is my love,
My love is my pain.

And you, you are the cause of all of it.

                                    Inspired by a friend.
                                    1-12-99

And So It Rained

As it rains the water washes over me, cleansing my spirit and renewing my soul.

My heart feels glad once again as I drift with the wind. Peace is searching for me once more and the calm surrounds me and holds me close. Although I know that the storm did not end in a day, it is a blessing to know that everything will certainly end.

I no longer hide from the gray clouds. Instead I embrace them and travel this journey with them into the sun.

This is the beginning of my healing processes and therefore I welcome the rain, I stand with the storm and let it move me, consume me, renew me.

The lightning will strike and bury this shell in the ground and I will blossom once more back into the beauty flower I once was.

I must understand that this too is just a cycle and I to must go through it.

I was born, I was raised, I learned, and I conquered, I have fallen, and I have been pushed. But I am strong and will always get back up.

This is my awakening, alone I was placed here and alone I will be removed, all that is placed in between will come and go, some will rise, while others fall, but in the end I stand alone.

No longer will I let another break what was given to me by a power stronger than us all.

I am a queen, I am a mother, I am a daughter, a sister, and a lover.

I am strong, brave, intelligent, and wise.

I am divine, I am an enigma.

I am so much more than what is seen on the day to day but yet I am still human therefore I am still vulnerable, I too can still be hurt and my heart can be broken . . .

And so it rained, so I rise, letting it wash away all the tears and all the sadness, while feeding the love and the light that is within me.

Dreams

The Dance

They dance at twilight on a Moonbeam.
They kiss at dawn on a Sunray.
They make love on a cloud & play with the Stars.
Mother Earth smiles & father Time has a Ball.

I.	He loves the rain.
	She loves the sun.

II.	She is the rain.
	He is the sun.

III.	They weep for each other.
	They laugh with each other.

IV.	They make love on the clouds.
	They rest in the sky.

V.	Be thankful for the rain.
	Bow down for the sun.

VI.	Sing with the angels.
	Dance with the stars.

VII.	Emerge with the world.
	Become one with the universe.

VIII.	Love your brother & sister, all colors.
	Educate all the children, all ages.

IX.	Smile forever.
	Cry no more.

X.	May peace be with you.
	May all things good come your way.

Revised 1/2011

Time

TIME DRIFTS BY,
    DOWN OFF THE PLAINS OF MY MIND.
IT SLOWLY PASSES,
    THROUGH THE CORRIDORS OF MY HEART.
WITHIN MY SOUL,
    IT LAYS ITS SEED.
PASSION & DESTRUCTION,
    GROWS FROM WITHIN THESE.
TIME CONSUMES MY LIFE,
    KILLING MY EMOTIONS SLOWLY.
BREAKING DOWN MY RESISTANCE,
    TEARING MY SPIRIT APART WHOLLY.
TIME BECOMES DEATH,
    AN ETERNITY OF PLEASURE & PAIN.
DEATH BECOMES ME,
    TAKING OVER MY BRAIN.
TIME DRIFTS BY,
    SLOWLY . . . QUICKLY.
TIME PASSES LIFELESS & SENSELESS,
    UNCARING TO MY NEEDS . . .

9/16/98

Hope is,

*We as strong black children so we need to look forward as we stand tall and keep our heads up high. Our struggle will be legendary in the books of their history that will tell of our future and story. We are burdened with a curse as well as a blessing; the color of our skin. The black ties that bond us together as well as the black lines that brings the bad weather. The railroads our people worked on will be the ones we shall cry "**Freedom** "upon on our dawn. The cotton fields they slaved in will be the ones we shall burn for all our African Americans, as our men and women dance within. Our underground railroads will rise up to be known,*

"Thou shall fear no man in this land that we built with our hands."

As we the next generation rise up and stand strong, we inherit their wisdom and pain that lasted so long. But as we listen to their cries and tears we must also remember their laughs & cheers. For yes we do hear them but can we hear each other, can we hear the cries of our sisters or see the pain of our brothers? Hope is we the next generation of a powerful society, and it will all come to be when we rise up and see. When we all stand up as one, you & me, my sisters & your brothers, our fathers & mothers. We will see hope as eternity and our love will rise up for all to see. For we are black, African Americans, Negroes, people, but we are noting if we can't love each other, if I can't love you and you can't love me . . .

The End

97'

Expectations

The expectations that are bestowed upon you at birth are the aspirations that will beckon you through life.

As you begin your journey into the unknown, you will learn about yourself and realize the true meaning of you.

As you reach for a higher state of mind, the thoughts of your mind, body, and soul will twine and become one.

They will turn into a precious heart that will carry you through an unknown parallel dimension of psychological, spiritual, and physical well being.

Then you will come forth to an astrological self-awareness that will welcome you into a galaxy of phenomenal proportions.

These will be the many parts to the book of yours, mine, and every other intelligent beings life.

Yes though everyone is beckon to be great many will fail in their journey, but the few that makes it through to the true Garden of Eden will know true self enlightenment for they will have stood their ground and fought their battle true.

They have faced not only the demons of the world, but also the demon of themselves.

They will have broke down all barriers preventing them from becoming one, one with the world, and with the universe, and one within themselves . . .

I am my sisters' keeper yes,

But I am the only one who can climb to the mountain top for me.

So if this mountain be great, so shall I . . .

Destiny

To what do you owe this world or to what does this world owe you.

Being alive is a gift, but to live is a curse.

Arise and realize that all things in some way change.

Time stops and the world stands still but the thought still remains the same.

I am one, but we are many, together we can accomplish plenty.

I spy devilish things with mine eye.

Devastating corruption, seducing mental eruptions of sane thoughts and all that's clear.

Psychological entities entering, feeding off the memories ultimately drives you insane.

Be that as it may you strayed so far away.

Letting go of the security of thing, which was taught to you.

Holding on to the unstable thoughts of the thoughts you thought for yourself.

Dance eternally with the trees
Play soulfully with the wind
Breathe in deep & sigh
Then say bye-bye

5/22/00

Desperation

1st   *lonely, oh so very lonely*
the deepest depths of loneliness
the dark solitary corridors of the mind
pain, agony, devotion

2nd   *time, endless time an eternity*
a prison within a prison, within the mind
labyrinths of the spirit
door of the soul

1st   *screams, cries, tears*
pain upon pain, upon pain
nightmares, torturing realities

2nd   *we hide in fright from horrors*
terrifying truths back us in corners
screams echoes through our ears

1st   *destruction, emptiness, pain, eternal*
agony, torturing innocence, oppressed
negativity

2nd   *hate upon hate, love within love*
time everlasting, eternity
desperation

10/26-27/98

Time
Space &
Time

I. MY PAIN HAS FINALLY TAKEN OVER, THE SWEET SURRENDER IS NOW UPON ME, MADNESS HAS FINALLY TAKEN OVER MY SOUL THE END IS NEAR, I SHALL NOT FEAR FOR MY HEART IS STILL COLD.

II. DEATH COMES SOFTLY TO MY HEART THE TIME PASSES, THE TIME WANDERS & WE SLOWLY START TO FALL APART THE EARTH ENGULPS MY SPIRIT IN ONE BREATHE THE WINDS BLOW, NOW NOTHINGS LEFT.

III. I MELT INTO THE FIRES & TASTE THE FRUITS OF THE UNIVERSE WE FEAST WITH THE STARS, DANCE WITH THE PLANETS BUT ONLY I HURT.

IV. I RISE AND YOU SLIP THROUGH MY FINGER TIPS, I FALL AND THERE YOU SIT, TAKE MY HANDS & CARESS MY LIPS, TOUCH MY SOUL & BE FOREVER IN MY MIND.

V. SLOWLY, GO SLOWLY SWIM THROUGH THE WANDERING SEAS, TRAVEL THE LONELY ROADS, WALK THE QUIET PATHS . . . SEE THE WORD THROUGH NEW EYES, TASTE THE UNKNOWN TRUTHS, BANSIH EVERYDAY LIES.
SEE ME
    I SEE YOU
FEEL ME
    I FEEL YOU
TAKE MY HAND AND LET US JOURNEY TOGETHER
    LET US TRAVEL TO THE UNIVERSE CORE
TOGETHER THERE'S NOTHING WE
    CAN'T ENDURE.

8/7/98

To The Enemy who
Escape the Weary
Eye ♦♦

Silent tears for a soft demise the end does come with a soft whimper yes, but a loud roar seems to set in the best.
To the weary and miserable, lonely and depressed. This call goes out to you, our hearts are all open so now you can rest.
For all the enemies who escaped your tear drenched eyes, the destruction shall cease, their prejudice shall fade, because hate is no longer tolerated it's time to make it better for our children lives.
To bring forth a better day, we all must make a better way, to bring forth a brighter child.
For over two hundred years our families have been oppressed my innocent dears.
For over two hundred years our people have been broken down, dreams have been shattered & spirits have been killed, innocence is now lost & more blood is being spilled.
Open your eyes for the problems are right at hand.
Open your hearts for the solutions are in every woman & man.
Break down the barriers of all the ignorant minds, lets reach for all human kind.
To all the enemies who escape the weary eye, the time is now for us to win; the future is here so the hate must now end.

The End

97'

Tragedy

Tragedy comes to us all in many forms, it engulfs us fully and destroy our will to be, to become.

It takes away our very existence, slowly eating away at our souls, patiently tearing us apart.

Tragedy seeps in through love and breaks us down gently.

It caresses our pain, with sadness and seduces us with destruction.

Tragedy, unbearable by any other name, we are apart of it, and it is a part of us.

It's the things we shy away from, the terrors that Terrifies us, the fears, we fear.

A

Terrifying

Reality,

Agonizing

Grieve an

Enigma

Desolate

Yearning

TRAGEDY

10/1/98

A Caged Bird

A caged bird cannot fly,
    so it sings it's sweet songs, so
it will not die.
A caged bird may cry,
    for its homesick for its family
even if it had a chance to say bye.
So for my beautiful caged bird
    keep your head held high.
For one day soon you'll
    be able to fly and fly.

I . . . Am . . . Madness!

M! A! D! N! E! SS! Madness

It consumes me engulfs me rape and abuse me

It is the everlasting torture of a love gone wrong a disease destined to destroy

It is the soft touch of a predator wrapped in silk a venomous beast poisoning my very soul

It is light and darkness the hysterical laughter and the incontrollable tears

It is the fear that paralyzes you the doubt that controls you the boulder beating down upon you

It is the mirror image of yourself broken shattered and destroyed

It is the shadows on the ceiling and the writing on the walls

It is the nightmares that keep you up at night the everlasting rollercoaster of destruction from the seduction of the corrupting eruption from the one you love

It is you sad simple beaten and weak a shell of what you once were the end result of the worlds pain

Madness it is the beginning middle and end

It is endless and eternal the most addictive sin . . .

I have walked a long and sometimes lonely road to reach the point where I stand today. Each poem within this collection is just a tiny piece of me that I would like to share with the world. There are happy memories and sad memories all wrapped up within these pages. Yet there are lessons learned within the words that I think have made me better, wiser, and stronger.

As I close the end of this chapter of the novel which is me, I would like to once again say thank you to all that stood by me, supported me and believed in me. For everyone that doubted or thought they could stop me, here I still stand and this is not the end, but a powerful beginning. There is so much I have to say and so much I have to give. So get ready world, now that I have started I will not be stopping. So I hope you receive what I have to offer and welcome that what I have to share . . .

VS Bryant

Printed in the USA
CPSIA information can be obtained
at www.ICGtesting.com
LVHW050245111223
766163LV00009B/617